Praise for *Stop Fear from Stopping You*

"In such uncertain times, I'm grateful that Dr. Odessky has come out with this new book to help you tame your fears and live a fuller, calmer life where you are able to handle whatever comes your way. Join the thousands of others her words have helped and decide to take control. Start today. Start now."

—Dr. John Duffy, author of *Parenting the New Teen in the Age of Anxiety*

"When you're anxious, all you can see is your anxiety. It feels urgent, serious and overwhelming. You wonder if you'll always feel this way. You wonder, Why me? Why now? Why won't it stop? You feel frustrated and hopeless—like there's nothing you can do. Thankfully, there is. There are many strategies to help manage and minimize anxiety... excellent ideas from the new book...written by Helen Odessky, PsyD, a clinical psychologist who specializes in anxiety and also struggled with it herself."

—PsychCentral

T0124678

STOP
FEAR
FROM
STOPPING
YOU

How to Overcome Your Fears So You Can Make Decisions with Confidence, Conquer Obstacles, and Go After What Really Matters

STOP
FEAR
FROM
STOPPING
YOU

The Art and Science of Becoming Fear-Wise

DR. HELEN ODESSKY

author of *Stop Anxiety from Stopping You*

mango
PUBLISHING GROUP
CORAL GABLES

Stop Fear from Stopping You: The Art and Science of Becoming Fear-Wise

Library of Congress Cataloging-in-Publication number: 2019954734

ISBN: (print) 978-1-64250-242-8, (ebook) 978-1-64250-243-5

BISAC category code: SEL024000—SELF-HELP / Self-Management / Stress Management

Printed in the United States of America

To Maya and Alex

TABLE OF CONTENTS

Foreword

By Dr. John Duffy

Fear has been gripping the hearts and minds of millions of people since the beginning of time. There are so many things we find ourselves scared of: spiders, heights, small talk, and even new relationships. Fear influences us in ways that we don't even realize until it's too late. At times, fear stops us from even starting the process of accomplishing our goals. We were not meant to live in this constant state of fear.

In such uncertain times, I'm grateful that Dr. Odessky has come out with this new book to help you tame your fears and live a fuller, calmer life where you are able to handle whatever comes your way. In this compelling guide, Dr. Odessky has all the tools you'll need to finally look fear in the face and let it know you aren't going to let it rule your life. Join the thousands of others her words have helped and decide to take control. Start today. Start now.

I was fortunate enough to read Dr. Helen Odessky's first book, *Stop Anxiety from Stopping You*, and my reflections on it ring true again for this latest work.

"Read this book, and you will find everything you need to beat anxiety once and for all. It's not a trick, or a quickie one-off. Instead, it is a comprehensive, easy-to-apply system for anxiety eradication. Keep this book close. Take your time and work through it. Trust Helen to guide you through. It will change your life. It will free you. Finally."

"Nothing in life is to be feared, it is only to be understood. Now is the time to understand more, so that we may fear less."

—Marie Curie

Introduction

A Note to the Reader

"The future does not belong to the fainthearted, it belongs to the brave."

—Ronald Reagan, Address to the Nation on *Challenger*

Dear reader,

As I write this book, the world is gripped by fear. Economic, social, health, and other fears have intensified in the face of a global health pandemic. While it is currently consuming the headlines of major news outlets, fear is certainly not a novel phenomenon. To fear, even to fear greatly, is unequivocally human. And, while fear is part of our nature, so is courage. When we begin to understand our fears and what they are about, we can harness them. When we acknowledge, accept, and act with purpose in the face of fear, we become fear-wise.

Unlike fearlessness, which operates under the illusion that no danger exists, being fear-wise creates a processing system for fear. Being fear-wise serves three important functions. First, it allows us to deal with fears in a more realistic fashion and calls for decisions and action in the absence of absolute safety or certainty. Next, it fosters a climate of developing creative solutions to address our problems. Finally, it allows us to hold on to faith and hope which, while not sufficient in and of themselves, are necessary to help us implement and course-correct in the areas of our lives we need it most. Specifically, at work, in relationships, and how we conduct our lives—when we encounter failure, rejection, or defeat, and when our circumstances challenge us to aim higher.

This book focuses on personal fears that we face when we are in situations or periods of our lives that test us. Whether at work or in personal relationships, fears often show up as insecurity, difficulty with decision making, and feeling immobilized. These fears stand in the way of us experiencing fulfillment academically, derail our success at work, and block us from experiencing joy and satisfaction in our relationships. If we work through these fears and develop a fear-wise stance, we can open the door to greater purpose, accomplishment, and true intimacy.

Ultimately, we must all confront the challenges of life with both fear and courage. We all have some areas in life where we are more afraid and others where we show more courage. The good news is that courage is a muscle that we can build and develop.

When we learn to address our fears and choose courage, we become fear-wise. In order to do so, we can practice the AAA model: Acknowledge, Accept, and Act with Purpose. First, we have to acknowledge whether the fear we feel is giving us the signal about something that is life-threatening or whether the threat is to our ego. Next, we have to accept our current set of circumstances and feelings. Finally, we have to decide to take purposeful action; being fear-wise is not a spectator sport. Becoming fear-wise is a process. Change is usually incremental rather than drastic or categorical. In the process of becoming fear-wise, the following steps are essential.

THE FEAR-WISE STEPS

1. The Fear-Wise Learn to Give Up Their Excuses

Excuses are shields of armor to protect us from facing what is truly difficult. Even as we make excuses publicly or privately, there is a part of us that knows we are lying. Aim to speak and acknowledge the truth to yourself and give up your excuses. For example, if your excuse is "I have not started dating after my divorce because I have not lost the twenty pounds I need to lose," you may want to acknowledge that the reason you have not started to date again is that it feels too vulnerable and you are afraid of getting hurt.

Acknowledging your excuses allows you to solve the real problem—your fear of trusting someone else and the vulnerability you feel regarding entering the dating world after all these years. Being able to look at the real problem may be more painful, but it offers you a gift of creating a path forward— emotionally healing after your divorce. Only by acknowledging the truth can we create change.

2. The Fear-Wise Give Up Perfectionism

I hate to be the bearer of bad news, but I have to be brutally honest here—no amount of hard work will land you a perfect relationship, a perfect career, or a perfect life. All we can aim for is creating a good-enough life filled with opportunity to get our needs met and to experience joy. Idealizing and expecting perfection gets in the way of both and often eclipses the good that is already in our lives. I am not asking you to settle for less-than here.

This is not about making concessions regarding things that you consider non-negotiable. It is about finding a way forward that is attainable and offers an opportunity for success. Perfection is the opposite of that—it is a trap—a shiny hollow object that fuels the ego but leaves our soul empty. Let go of your desire for perfection in favor of excellence and the good enough.

3. The Fear-Wise Accept Fear as Part of the Equation

Have you ever tried to not be afraid? If you have, you know that it is absolutely futile. Fear is, at times, inevitable, and it is not fear that counts, but what we do with it. I encourage you to listen to what your fear is telling you and act with it. It is going to be part of the picture regardless of what we do sometimes, and it will also fuel us to get the job done. Whether it is to start dating, go for that promotion, or challenge ourselves in a myriad of other ways, fear will often walk alongside us—let it, and move forward with courage.

You may notice that some steps will be easier for you to accomplish and others may take you more time to hone and fine-tune. Stay with the process, practice being kind and patient with yourself, and keep going!

"Let me assert my firm belief that the only thing we have to fear is fear itself-nameless, unreasoning, unjustified terror which paralyzes needed efforts..."

—Franklin Delano Roosevelt, *First Inaugural Address*

Chapter 1

The Fear Grip

Fear (noun): "An unpleasant often strong emotion caused by anticipation or awareness of danger."

Fear (verb): "To be afraid of or expect with alarm."

—Merriam-Webster's Dictionary

Fear, although we all experience it, has been notoriously difficult to describe. To add to the confusion, we regularly use the term "fear" interchangeably with "anxiety." Dr. Aaron Beck, the founder of cognitive therapy, differentiated them in the following way: "Fear...is the appraisal of danger; anxiety is an unpleasant feeling [or] state evoked when fear is stimulated." Fear is the expectation, a thinking phenomenon, while anxiety is the resulting feelings fear evokes. However, fear does not have to result in anxiety. It can be a call to action, a mandate to respond.

There are three ways we can respond to fear: freeze (do nothing), take flight (avoid), or fight (exert force to counter the problem). These responses are mediated by the amygdala, a part of the brain, which is thought to be responsible for recognizing, experiencing, and expressing fear (Adolphs, 2013). As a survival strategy, it is thought that these responses serve to keep us safe and protected from threats. If you freeze, the predator may not notice you. If you flee, you can escape from the predator. Finally, if you are bigger or stronger, you can fight the predator and ensure your survival.

While adaptive from an evolutionary perspective, when it comes to our deepest fears, freezing and avoiding do not get us what we desire. When was the last time you heard someone say: "The way I got my dream job is by spending hours and hours daydreaming about it?" Avoiding is also unlikely to get us the career, relationships, or other goals we have set for ourselves. Have you ever had a friend who was hesitant to date tell you, "I just do not know where to meet someone." This friend was experiencing freeze mode. Freeze mode is lack of movement in any direction and it looks like paralysis of action. While in freeze mode, there is usually a frenzy of mental activity; however, this activity is circular and does not lead to decisions or action. Avoidance, or flight mode, looks like distancing or distracting yourself from the problem.

While freezing is the pathway to regret, avoidance is the pathway to anxiety. We tend to regret missed opportunities or roads not taken, and rarely can we fool ourselves into believing that by avoiding necessary risks, we will feel better in the long term. When we avoid important aspects of our lives routinely, we tend to lose confidence in ourselves and in our abilities. We also develop anxiety; we become increasingly afraid of the things we have been avoiding. While we all avoid doing unpleasant things from time to time, avoidance is a temporary salve, best applied sparingly.

Fight, the third response to fear, is more complex. If we use the energy of fighting to resist thoughts or feelings, we generally end up worse off for it. Imagine trying to convince yourself that your least favorite meal, the one that you dread and find disgusting, is absolutely delicious. To imagine it is one thing, but to truly feel it is nearly impossible—manufacturing feelings is an exhausting trap. Using our energy to fight our feelings will only expend our energy rather than getting us to overcome them. Fortunately, there is another option—we can look at the term "fight" as a means to action. If we define fight as purposeful action toward our goal, we can develop and exercise courage as we face our fears.

COURAGE

Courage: mental or moral strength to venture, persevere, and withstand danger, fear, or difficulty.

—Merriam-Webster's Dictionary

Courage. The very word brings up images of war heroes, bravery, sacrifice in the face of danger, and a host of other removed and largely unachievable hypothetical scenarios that most of us have not personally dealt with. It can also bring up feelings of guilt and shame: guilt about not having lived up to a principle we value and shame about not measuring up to an ideal and feeling "less than."

In discussing courage, there is danger in sounding moralistic or idealistic. However, the courage I am talking about is not some abstract spiritual or theological virtue, a brave act, or a badge of honor. The way I look at it, courage is not so much about rescuing a kitten from a rooftop as it is about getting up another day to face our challenges and obstacles. It is about leading our lives from a place of intention and purpose. In my research regarding what makes up courage, all definitions point to action as a constant. Here are some definitions that exemplify this concept:

"The strengths that make up courage reflect the open eyed exercise of will toward the worthy ends that are not certain of attainment."

—Martin E Seligman, PhD

"Courage is not the absence of fear, but rather the assessment that something else is more important than fear."

—Franklin D. Roosevelt

A few years ago, my husband and I were vacationing in Jamaica. We stayed at a lovely resort which was staffed by wonderful personnel who would go out of their way to speak to everyone. One evening, we were particularly impressed by the performance of the dance crew and began a conversation with a young man who performed that night. He was relaxed and friendly, at once charged up by the performance he had just finished and yet fully present and calm at the same time. We started chatting about his life in Jamaica, and he shared one of the most courageous stories I have ever heard.

Jonathan was born and grew up in the slums of Jamaica. His world seemed so small that it was hard to envision life anywhere else as he was growing up. The slums were overrun by the rule of drug lords, and as Jonathan got older, he saw his future dissipate in the life at the slums. When he was thirteen, he

was approached by the drug lords and ordered to sell drugs for
them. He managed to run away and hide from them, but this
was just one of many of their "requests." The following year, at
age fourteen, he was approached again. When he refused, yet
again, a gun was pointed at him and he was told that he was
going to lose his legs if he did not obey. Angry and desperate,
Jonathan shouted out, "Shoot me—I will never work for you!"

Jonathan said he did not know how he managed speak with
such defiance—he didn't even have the time to think his words
through—but the drug lords let him go. As a matter of fact, he
was thrown out of the slums and told that if he ever returned, he
and his family would all be brutally murdered. Jonathan spent
the rest of his teenage years running with a dance crew, training
and perfecting his routines for hours each day while trying to
survive on his own. The effort paid off in spades. As soon as he
reached adulthood, he was hired by a large corporation that
staffed resorts with dance talent.

As Jonathan described it, life in the slums made him very
angry, and seeing no hope for the future, he was always on
edge and ready to explode. Dancing made it necessary to learn
a new set of skills—discipline, emotional regulation and stress
management were just a few. He needed to become focused,
skilled, and dedicated. And that he did. This mild-mannered
young man worked hard and was at peace with himself and
his choices.

When we asked Jonathan what made him stand up to the drug lords, he shrugged his shoulders.

"I knew I could not live like that—that's all." He smiled the biggest smile I have ever seen, his eyes sparkling. That day, his act of courage got him out of being stuck in the slums, offered him a future, and secured his freedom. These days, his life is all about movement. It is a life filled with choices and possibilities.

Chapter 2

The Fear of Making the Wrong Choice

"Ditch the dream and be a doer, not a dreamer. Maybe you know exactly what it is you dream of being, or maybe you're paralyzed because you have no idea what your passion is. The truth is, it doesn't matter. You don't have to know. You just have to keep moving forward. You just have to keep doing something, seizing the next opportunity, staying open to trying something new. It doesn't have to fit your vision of the perfect job or the perfect life. Perfect is boring and dreams are not real."

—Shonda Rhimes, Dartmouth Commencement Address, 2014

DECIDE TO DECIDE:
THE PRICE OF INDECISION

A popular joke in graduate school when it came time to write that dreaded dissertation project was that everyone's house became a lot more organized and tidy. The dreaded chore of deep cleaning suddenly became increasingly appealing because it did not involve long hours of sitting by the computer and working on the tedious tasks of data gathering, writing a literature review, or finding the right words to present your conclusions. Since this particular graduate program specialized in producing clinicians, not academics, the career-building appeal of a dissertation, which can be motivational in other academic settings, was lost on most students. Few would use it to begin a career in academia, pivot this initial attempt into a publication for future research, or have it go beyond the confines of this particular graduate institution. To most students, this project was a matter of fulfilling a school requirement—no more, no less.

Most of us also had fairly busy lives outside of our academic classes, including being employed part- or full-time and accruing clinical hours required for licensure during part-time or full-time positions. This was in addition to trying to navigate family, personal relationships, and other responsibilities we all had. The price of not working on this project meant incurring large expenses while delaying your graduation. To make matters even more complicated, if your graduation was delayed, it meant putting off full-time, paid work opportunities that were only accessible once you graduated and which led to the necessary accrual of licensing hours post-graduation that would enable you to sit for the licensing exam. Thus, any interruption incurred significant costs of time, energy, and money on both the front end and the back end because it ultimately delayed entry into the field we were so hungry to enter by delaying our pathway to licensure.

There was a group of students who did not appear to make the decision to comply with the requirement. Instead, when everyone would chat about balancing their various commitments, these students would offer vague answers and explanations about what they were doing. This usually sounded like "I am taking my time" or "I ran into some difficulties" followed by a change of subject. There was a lack of energy and these students seemed to be heading into this project without a plan, hoping against hope that something would eventually spontaneously materialize.

Unfortunately for that group of students, the decision to commit to this project fully had to be made and steps to move it forward had to be taken regularly. We knew that, for them, failing to plan equaled planning to fail, because arrangements had to be made ahead of time for the senior academic staff to review drafts and to meet deadlines set forth by the school. Despite the reality that the significant costs of graduate education meant that the majority of students were taking sizeable student loans that only increased their debt if the project was not completed on time, these students were immobilized. It was clear that the heft of this decision caused these students great distress, and unfortunately for them, inaction came with a hefty price tag.

It was not that these students intentionally decided to spend more money and to put off starting their career for an extra year or two. On the contrary, while they were deciding whether or not they could or should take on the project and the timeline, time passed and the decision was made for them by the circumstances. In essence, their lack of action was also a decision. The fear of making a decision can look like inaction, passivity, incessant information gathering, lengthy lists of pros and cons, and many other displays that are designed to create delay with busyness or distraction. It can also look like endless discussions that center around the same topic and do not result in any action planning. It looks like spinning your wheels and feels like you are treading water or are stuck in the mud.

What Is Really Going On?

In my professional experience, we generally fear the following things when we fear making a decision. First, we fear making an imperfect decision. Second, we fear judgment about the decision we are about to make. Finally, we fear the regret that we may feel if our decision turns out unfavorably and the difficulty we will have in forgiving ourselves should that happen. Let's look at each of these concerns in more detail.

Making a perfect decision can be a daunting proposition. Because all decisions have a profile of costs and benefits, we are usually faced with selecting between a few imperfect alternatives. In each scenario, we are likely to lose out on something that may be appealing to us and to select an option that has significant drawbacks. By definition, then, all of our decision-making yields imperfect decisions. To make matters even more complicated, in hindsight, these drawbacks may even appear to have been predictable because we now know how the specific decision turned out, a benefit we do not have at the outset.

If all of our decisions are imperfect, then the criteria have to be changed to making good-enough decisions instead of perfect ones. Acting otherwise sets us up for discontent at best and feelings of failure at worst. Decide to make an imperfect decision in order to free yourself from the clutches of perfectionism. Consider your decision as a point on a data line, not an absolute. Few decisions—other than detonating nuclear warheads or having a child—are irrevocable. Of course, some decisions take longer to deliberate on. We would be wise to be selective and engage in a longer scouting process when finding a suitable partner for marriage or committing to a career. One the other hand, selecting a new coffee maker for our home or a place to vacation are decisions that are best addressed fairly swiftly.

Fearing judgment can also get us stuck when it comes to making important decisions. Recently, I worked with Samantha, a very bright, Ivy League-educated young woman who was becoming increasingly dissatisfied with her career in the corporate world. Although her job compensated her well and offered an intellectual challenge, it lacked the opportunity for her to make the type of impact she longed to make in the world. Her dream was to become a medical doctor, and while she was clear that this was something she unequivocally wanted to pursue, she was concerned about being judged as foolish. Leaving a lucrative career path in the corporate world to pursue a career in medicine is certainly not for everyone, but she was clear, and so we had to address her fear of judgment. "This judgment," I asked her, "whose judgment is it—what people are you worried about specifically?" She shrugged her shoulders, paused, and stared blankly for a moment before answering. "I guess I can't think of anyone specifically—perhaps it is my own judgment and worry about what people might think."

This insight allowed Samantha to take charge and move forward with her decision. As is true for most of us, Samantha projected some of what she was afraid of onto what she thought other people might think. While we cannot guarantee that someone will not judge our career choice, we also have no control over this. What we do control are the self-judgments we take on. I encouraged Samantha to own wholeheartedly what she truly believed was her path, a career in medicine, and to let everything else fade. By keeping her goal in focus, Samantha came up with a plan for a transition into her new career that fit with what she thought was best for her.

Managing regrets is the final obstacle to making decisions. Let's be frank—it is impossible to foresee exactly how a decision will play out due to multiple circumstances outside of our control. As we look back, sometimes we piece together a picture that looks quite different due to the extra information we have acquired through our experience. At the time of the decision being made, this information is usually inaccessible. In spite of this, I believe that good decision-making can happen if we allow ourselves to be solely responsible for managing only the known variables in the equation. If we make a decision that does not turn out favorably for us, we still have a choice as to how we manage feelings of regret.

Most people seek to minimize losses, and so it is natural that we go to great lengths to minimize regrets. In my experience, we tend to regret the avenues we did not purse, the tasks we did not take on, and the words we did not say more than what we actually chose to do. In other words, we regret our inaction, passivity, and avoidance more than we regret our actions. Sometimes, it is hard to remember that when we are staring in the face of a decision, but I encourage you to keep it top of mind.

For those of us prone to regret, commit to a non-blaming stance toward your own actions. Use the opportunity to re-evaluate in an information-gathering session to see if there is anything that can be taken away or learned from a bad outcome and resist the urge to blame. Notice your self-talk and use a compassionate voice to really consider if there is anything to be gained by beating yourself up. Usually, there is only guilt and shame that go along with self-blame. If this is your preferred mode of speaking to yourself, I encourage you to change it in favor of a gentler one. There is a world of difference between holding yourself accountable through self-honesty and self-monitoring and brutally tearing yourself down following any perceived mistake or difficult situation.

To interrupt the blame and shame cycle, try to speak to yourself kindly by focusing on the facts of the situation. Decide to resist any name-calling or insisting that "you should have known" something that was simply unknown to you at the time. Acknowledge your feelings about the situation by naming them. Are you feeling discouraged, disappointed, shocked, hurt, frustrated, embarrassed, ashamed, sad, angry, afraid, or something else? Allow yourself to feel your feelings without harsh words of admonishment and remind yourself of your ability to weather setbacks. Take away the lessons to be learned, if there are any, and discard everything else. Challenge yourself to feel hope in your abilities to get through a difficult point and to pivot in another direction, while accepting the circumstances of your current situation.

When faced with a decision, the fear-wise acknowledge the following truths:

1. They know that lack of action is a decision.

2. They decide to decide.

3. They make room for error.

4. They create their contingency plans based on input, not fear.

5. They see decisions as points on a data line, not as absolutes.

6. They minimize undue blame and regret.

Fear-Wise Truth: Lack of action, a decision passively deferred or ignored, is a decision in and of itself.

"Success is not final, failure is not fatal, the courage to continue is what counts."

—Winston Churchill

Chapter 3

The Fear of Failure

"I have learned that failure is really God's way of saying, 'Excuse me, you're moving in the wrong direction.' "

—Oprah Winfrey, Wellesley Commencement Address, 1997

Few fears get us stuck as mightily as the fear of failure. This fear is typically communicated in two ways. Most people acknowledge it head-on and say that they are afraid to fail. Occasionally, I hear the opposite, "I am afraid of success." In my experience, fear of success is a myth. It is a more palatable way of expressing that I am afraid I will not attain success. This fear of success is really a shell, the fear of failure masking itself as something else. Are we really afraid of too much money falling from the sky and finding ourselves in the difficult predicament of spending it? No, we are afraid of the flipside, the lack of success that our efforts produce. That lack of success is what we find dispiriting, frightening and daunting—and it holds us hostage more than we care to admit.

And, precisely because we do not like to admit it, we create a shield or a whole-body armor of excuses to protect ourselves. These excuses are self-sustaining and they create an ecosystem that protects us from acknowledging just how afraid we are. Here is a list of what some of these excuses may sound like:

- I would love to be in a relationship, but I come from a broken home, and I just do not think I am built for having a family.

- I have already wasted so much time being stuck in bad relationships—it is really too late to start over.

- I would have loved to run a marathon, if only I had smaller hips, was a little thinner, more athletic, or in better shape.

- I would love to travel more, but I just did not grow up in a family that travelled.

- I would love to go to college if only I had more time to study.

- I would love to go after my dreams, but I am just too busy with my current responsibilities as it is.

- I would love to pursue this particular hobby (music, dance, acting, etc.) but I was told I am just not good at it.

- I have always dreamed of doing something great with my life, but I am just too old to try at this point.

- I think my childhood really did a number on me; I do not think I will be able to get anywhere I want to be.

- I just do not have the luck that other people seem to have.

- It is all about connections in this world, and I do not seem to have any good ones.

- Some people are dreamers; I seem to be better at imagining rather than going for it.

- I lack the success gene, always have.

- There are just no jobs in a bad economy.

- If only I had chosen a different career, spouse, job—I would be much happier now.

- I do not feel ready to change; I think I should wait and see.

- If something better was supposed to happen, it would have happened by now.

- I think other people are just naturally smarter, more driven, happier, more gifted, or talented than I am.

- Maybe I should just be happy with what I have and not push my luck.

- I could try, but it is just not worth it—what if I do not get what I want and end up just as unhappy?

The excuses above are just a few that I have heard over the years. Excuses are, of course, as infinite as our imagination allows. And they are self-reinforcing—for every one of these beliefs we hold, there is a supporting anecdote or story that we can recall fairly quickly reinforcing our idea wholeheartedly. What is striking to me is how quickly we use these beliefs to dismiss our most cherished dreams! It is truly a testament to the power of the fear of failure.

In her brilliant book *Mindset*, Dr. Carol Dweck delves into how our mindset determines how we view failure. Those of us with a "fixed mindset," the predilection to have our world categorically divided into set constructs, such as smart vs. dumb, see failure as an indication that we are somehow not good enough. Using a fixed mindset, we see failure as proof of our own inadequacy. It can drive us to lower our expectations just to protect ourselves from blows to our self-worth.

When we see failure as proof of who we are as people, we tend to fall into low stakes, low effort behavior. In turn, we develop learned helplessness, which is the phenomenon that leads us to believe we are less capable than we actually are and is also strongly associated with depression. As a result of this thinking, we seek opportunities that validate that we are not that bad versus striving to do better. We may also start to give up and to appear indifferent. We do this to ward off the feelings of shame and humiliation that follow our perceived defeat.

Fortunately, there is another alternative to a fixed mindset—a "growth mindset." People with this mindset see failure as an opportunity to grow or improve. Unlike people with a fixed mindset who retreat in the face of failure, people with a growth mindset actually get motivated by failure. It boosts their desire to keep going and to excel at their chosen task. People with a growth mindset tend to experience failure as something expected on the path to success, do not take it as a character flaw, and actually welcome it and find it energizing. A good example of someone with a growth mindset is Michael Jordan who famously focused on the player who upstaged him in the prior game in order to motivate himself to work harder and to up-level his own game. Dweck's findings are nothing short of amazing, considering most of us do not find failure invigorating.

Failure is not absolute, and often it ends up that failed attempts can lead us to the right opportunities. In college, I took a history class that included a trip to travel around Europe for two weeks. My travel documentation got delayed, and rather than being able to travel with the group of my peers, I wound up having my trip delayed and had to travel by myself internationally to catch up with the group. Since my tickets were re-booked last minute, I ended up travelling standby and had to find alternative modes of transportation to get to my destination. Although not without misadventures, this wrong turn taught me the skills of independence and self-reliance.

From Dr. Carol Dweck's research we can infer the importance of setting goals, both in the face of failure and as a way to combat our fear of it. Setting goals for yourself helps create accountability.

Use the goal chart below to help keep you on track. For every goal, write out what you are going to complete, using specific details so that you can measure your progress. For example, if your goal is to start an exercise program, rather than writing "I will exercise," describe what you are going to be doing and for how long you will be doing it.

"I will bike, hike or walk for thirty minutes three times per week, Monday, Wednesday and Friday at eight a.m." is a specific and measurable goal. Make sure you include when you are going to do a specific task and put it in your calendar. Set up a progress check in for yourself to make sure you are noticing and working through any obstacles that may be impeding your progress. Finally, set a completion date even if you plan to keep the goal going forward.

For example, if you intend to work out year-round, you would still set a goal for the month and check in at the end of the month to gauge your progress. This also helps you keep momentum going. Because goals are meant to be revised and reevaluated periodically, you may decide to continue exercising, but once you build up your stamina, you may set a new goal for yourself like running a 5K or training for a half marathon. Begin charting your goals with the chart on the following page.

GOAL CHART

My Specific Goal	Start Date	Progress	Completion Date
(Example: I will go to the gym three times per week during the month of January.)	(e.g. January 1)	(How is it going?)	(e.g. January 31)

Fear-Wise Plan

What steps can we take if we find that we tend to fall into a fixed mindset when it comes to failure? Try the following suggestions in the face of fear of failure and make it your fear-wise plan.

1. Embrace the task at hand. Create a specific plan, including what you are going to do, when you are going to do it, and how you are going to do it. Make sure to visualize yourself implementing this plan in vivid detail as you bring it to life.

2. Remember that we fail at tasks, not as people.

3. Practice good habits in the face of feeling lousy. Obstacles are unavoidable, so when you are faced with them and the negative emotions they produce, continue to take the positive steps that you know are likely to produce results.

4. Engage with your full effort. Low effort will not protect you from failure—it will secure it. Effort is what produces results—always.

5. Set goals, and then set slightly bigger and more challenging goals than those that make you comfortable. Goals that make you stretch are goals that keep you engaged.

6. Learn from criticism—constructive criticism offers us the opportunity to grow and improve. We all have blind spots, and feedback shines the light on those areas that need improvement.

7. Confront your own entitlement. People do not get ahead because they are inherently "special" or "talented," they get ahead because they commit to doing what is necessary, take responsibility, and prove themselves to be reliable.

8. Confront your denial of problems. If you deny your problems, no change or effort is required. You have to acknowledge what needs changing in order for growth to happen.

9. Look at the successes of others as inspiration. Other people's success does not diminish or threaten what you can achieve. Instead, it can embolden you to achieve even more than you thought possible.

10. Learn to fail gracefully. Failing is an art. We all fail and have to get back up and try it again. Do so without blaming and shaming yourself, and you will soon reap the benefits of failing.

THE UNFULFILLED POTENTIAL MYTH

"Continuous effort, not strength or intelligence is the key to unlocking our potential."

—Liane Cordes

How many times have we heard a variant of "He had such a bright future, but he just did not fulfill his potential!" What does this statement actually reveal about the way we see success and failure? I think it points to a fixed belief we may have about how much our endowments, intellectual or otherwise, dictate where we may end up in life.

I see the idea of unfulfilled potential as a destructive belief. I believe it is a faulty notion that only some of us have potential that we need to nurture. I would say that all of us have inherent potential that needs to be nurtured and that none of us are special solely on the basis of our potential. It is our efforts, our hard work, our perseverance through challenges, and a myriad of other factors that really determine our successes.

Our society promotes this myth of great potential and it sets us up for disappointment. Great potential is portrayed as an elusive unicorn in Hollywood movies, to be sought after, desired, and admired. It invites us to imagine that effortless

"The number one cause of unfulfilled potential is never deciding that NOW matters more than any other time in your life."

—Hal Elrod

success not only exists, but that it is also more desirable and somehow better than success that has been achieved through grit, hard work, and perseverance.

Let's think of it another way: would we want our children to believe that doing something well is only worthwhile if it comes easily? Would we encourage them to stick with tasks that they already know how to do perfectly just so that they could prove to themselves and others that they excel at effortless wins? What impact would this belief system have on their emotional and intellectual development? And, where would we be as a society in terms of our development or our ability to be able to continue to solve and resolve challenges that are increasingly novel, complex, and multi-dimensional?

It is a lie that we have been sold that ease and effortlessness are desirable attributes of success. Surely, we all crave some ease in our lives. But, just as importantly, we crave challenge and the desire to grow and improve. The myth of unfulfilled potential hampers us from powering through as though it is shameful to do so.

There is no shame in struggle. Our potential is dynamic and largely unknowable. The great unfulfilled potential trap limits us by implying that things should come easier than they actually can and that we have to prove that we still have this potential versus growing into it. I believe we all have some growing to do in our life, and when we stretch and grow is when we truly thrive and succeed.

So, if you find yourself in the thick of an unfulfilled potential story—here is what to do about it. Give up the notion that potential is a finite and foregone conclusion. Accept that there have been opportunities missed and steps not taken and forgive yourself for them. Simply let what is in the past remain there without taking the excuses or faulty beliefs that got you there into your future. Next, start charting your goals so that you can practice effortful success. Set specific deadlines, create accountability, and schedule regular check-ins to gauge your progress. Start seeing those efforts as worthwhile and give yourself credit for taking steps and working hard.

Getting back up after a failure is something that we all have to encounter. None of us would have ever learned how to walk if, as toddlers, we just gave up trying after a few falls. It is the ability to keep going that will determine your level of success after a setback. All of us will, at times, fail in our endeavors and do so many times if we lead full lives.

Sometimes, fear of failure is disguised as something else: shyness, laziness, slowness, etc. For instance, sometimes when we are afraid to fail in performance situations, trying not to score the winning shot looks like a missed opportunity or slow reflexes. If this resonates with you, I encourage you to really look at what you are protecting yourself from. Often, we are afraid of a bruised ego—nothing more, nothing less. But as the old saying goes, "nothing ventured, nothing gained."

We gain nothing by staying on the sidelines and letting others take the winning shot instead of us. So, let's get in the game! Get going—you have nothing to lose but a little hubris. You have a world of opportunities you can gain—and that is no small thing! Learning to go for it can be somewhat of a jagged curve. Sometimes it will come easy, and other times it may feel like a slog. Have compassion for yourself as you do this. Every time you try to go for it, give yourself the credit you deserve, regardless of outcome. And, every time you have a miss, be gentle with how you treat yourself. Encourage yourself to keep at it!

Fear-Wise Plan

The fear-wise acknowledge the following truths:

1. Fear of failure is natural—it shows us that something important to us is a stake.

2. What is at stake is not our self-esteem or self-respect—it is something we hope to achieve or accomplish.

3. In every failure, there is a lesson to be learned—look for it and discard the rest.

4. Failure is a bump on the road to anything that is worthwhile.

5. Success is neither necessary nor guaranteed, but it is the process that is always valuable.

6. There is no effortless success; we all have to work at what we achieve in this life—effortful success is worth it!

7. Potential is a dynamic construct—only you can decide how you will grow and evolve.

Chapter 4

The Fear of What Other People Think

"It is not the critic who counts; not the man who points out how the strong man stumbles, or where the doer of deeds could have done them better. The credit belongs to the man who is actually in the arena, whose face is marred by dust and sweat and blood; who strives valiantly; who errs, who comes short again and again, because there is no effort without error and shortcoming; but who does actually strive to do the deeds; who knows great enthusiasms, the great devotions; who spends himself in a worthy cause; who at the best knows in the end the triumph of high achievement, and who at the worst, if he fails, at least fails while daring greatly, so that his place shall never be with those cold and timid souls who neither know victory nor defeat."

—Theodore Roosevelt, "Citizenship in a Republic" speech

How many times have we all wasted our precious time worrying what other people may think of us? Whether it is wondering about our choice of dress or the career choices we make, from the car we drive to the neighborhood we live in, when our choices are dictated from a place of what our friends, neighbors, and even perfect strangers will think, we often settle for less-than, and we usually settle for someone else's choice.

We may become incessant information gatherers regarding what we *should* do and how we *should* lead our lives. We may begin to heavily edit and sensor what we say and offer only "safe" opinions, ones we are sure will be accepted. We may end up keeping our best ideas to ourselves, for fear of criticism and ridicule, and give up important parts of ourselves just to fit it with what is currently a popular opinion or trend.

Here is what it looks like when we worry too much about what people think:

- We hide our true thoughts and feelings and do not speak up regarding our opinions and preferences.

- We change aspects of our personality in order to fit in and end up acting like social chameleons.

- We become professional advice gatherers, seeking out affirmation for our life choices, no matter how small.

- We stop sharing news about ourselves; negative and even positive news becomes something we withhold.

- We take on perfectionistic attitudes in order to avoid judgment, criticism, or rejection.

- We often second-guess the decisions we make and repeatedly replay scenarios about what other people are thinking about us.

- We cover up anything that is unique or different about us in an effort to avoid negative judgment.

- We follow the crowd, even when we would truly prefer not to do so.

- We avoid certain people or situations because we become too uncomfortable that we are not able to say "no" or express our preferences.

Why do we do this? Look over the list below to see if any of the following sounds familiar:

- We are afraid of criticism. We would like to avoid being teased, judged, ridiculed, or shamed with regards to our choices.

- We want to make sure our choice is the "correct" or "right" one.

- We are used to making concessions and it has become a habit. Therefore, we do not state our preferences, even when we are asked.

- We dislike making our own choices, so we often lean on others in order to point us in the right direction.

- We dislike sticking out or being perceived as "different," so we tend to stick with what we perceive to be a "safe" choice.

- We lack trust in our own decision-making ability and crowdsource our decisions.

- We do not like conflict and so we often "go along to get along" and regret decisions we make after the fact.

Here's the fear-wise truth and what to do about it:

- Consider the fact that other people generally do not spend all that much time caring about what you choose to do and how you choose to live your life.

- Develop self-compassion for your own needs and tune into them regularly. Journaling is a great way to do this.

- Decide to let go of perfectionism in favor of the good-enough. This option creates a possibility for excellence and sets you up for success.

- Start being authentic in your relationships by expressing your sincere preferences and opinions regarding various issues.

- First do some introspection and prioritize your own values, then look for other like-minded people to find your tribe.

- Accept that being unique or different in some respects is okay. These differences have the potential to enrich and deepen your relationships and your life.

- Learn to say "no" and set boundaries with people around your time and what you choose to do.

- Acknowledge that you cannot control what other people think anyway, but you can always control what you do and how you decide to live your life.

"Who fears failure the most? People who have achieved something—people who are demonstrably *but* frauds."

—Amy Cuddy

Chapter 5

The Fear of Being an Impostor

"The beauty of the impostor syndrome is you vacillate between extreme egomania and a complete feeling of: 'I'm a fraud! Oh God they're onto me! I'm a fraud!'... just try to ride the egomania when it comes and enjoy it, and then slide through the idea of fraud."

—Tina Fey

In her famous Ted Talk "Your Body Language May Shape Who You Are" which has been viewed more than fifty million times, Amy Cuddy talked about her experience of feeling like an impostor. As a bright high school student, Amy was on track to get her doctorate degree from an elite university and on track to enter a career in academia.

Unfortunately, Amy was involved in a very serious car accident that caused significant brain damage and was told that her dream had to drastically change. Not only was she no longer a candidate for a Ph.D. program, it also looked like an undergraduate college degree was out of her reach. Amy worked hard to regain her strength, and she did make it to college. She not only made it to college, she made it to an Ivy League level Ph.D. program—and that is where she really felt like an impostor, someone who did not belong and was not supposed to be there. In fact, she felt it so strongly that she told one of her professors that she did not belong and was going to quit.

Fortunately for Amy, her professor would not hear of it and told her she was not allowed to give up. So, Amy continued in the program, all the while feeling like an impostor, like she was fooling everyone and she really did not belong there. She continued that way until she became a faculty member at another prestigious academic institution. As a professor, she had a student approach her and share her own fears that she did not think she belonged. It was at that moment that Amy Cuddy realized that she had overcome her imposter syndrome. She no longer felt this way. She had become the person who she felt she was faking being all along. And now, it was she who was telling a student to hang in there in the face of this fear.

Feeling like an impostor is a rather commonplace phenomenon. It is particularly common when we find ourselves starting a new career or role. High level executives, healthcare professionals, and attorneys frequently start wondering if they really belong, are being effective, or contributing as much they should. For some of us, these feelings are not just passing; they haunt us for years or even decades. They also carry a sense of secrecy and shame—a fundamental flaw of being not on par or not good enough. And, the more success we have, the more our shame seems to compound.

Interestingly enough, success is not a cure for the impostor syndrome, it just raises the stakes and stokes the fear of finally being discovered. In her bestselling book *Lean In,* Sheryl Sandburg, the Chief Financial Officer at Facebook, wrote:

> **"Every time I was called on in class, I was sure that I was about to embarrass myself. Every time I took a test, I was sure that it had gone badly. And every time I didn't embarrass myself—or even excelled—I believed that I had fooled everyone yet again. One day soon, the jig would be up... This phenomenon of capable people being plagued by self-doubt has a name—the impostor syndrome. Both men and women are susceptible to the impostor syndrome, but women tend to experience it more intensely and be more limited by it."**

Having worked with both men and women on this issue, I see it holding men back just as much as women. It looks different when women experience it—we tend to opt out altogether, falling into getting a safe job or resolving that a certain level of success is not achievable and leaning into our other roles. For men, fear of being an impostor tends to look more like treading water; waiting too long to go for that promotion, applying for positions where they do not have to stretch their set of skills too far. And both men and women suffer for it.

Amy Cuddy did overcome her fear, and the advice she shares is "Fake it till you become it." Instead of faking it until you make it, which just seems to grow the impostor fears—when we "make it," we just feel like the lie is getting bigger and our fears grow stronger. If we hang in there, if we just stay the course and act like we belong, eventually those behaviors can begin to shape our new views of ourselves—not as impostors, but as capable people who do belong there—because we have become that person. If we embody this concept, however, we do have to go through some important changes in our fear belief system.

Fear-Wise Beliefs

We can change our fear-based beliefs into fear-wise beliefs:

1. Unhelpful belief: "My being here is an accident." Instead, practice the helpful belief, "My being here is a result of hard work and the skillset that I possess."

2. Unhelpful belief: "My colleagues and management all routinely overestimate my abilities." Instead, practice the helpful belief, "My abilities are at or above the level of my work."

3. Unhelpful belief: "My previous achievements were just a stroke of dumb luck—a fluke." Instead, try the helpful belief, "My prior accomplishments were all well-deserved, and I have earned every single one of them."

4. Unhelpful belief: "People would be sorely disappointed if they really knew me." Instead, try the helpful belief, "People do really know me and they really value me."

5. Unhelpful belief: "I have been able to fool everyone and it is just a matter of time before I am discovered and labeled a 'fraud.'" Instead try the helpful belief: "I have fooled no one; other people accept my contributions for their merits."

Fear-Wise Truths

1. A novice is not an impostor, it is someone who needs
    to gather relevant experience and skills and who could
    benefit from some good mentorship. A novice is someone
    who is capable of growing into his or her role.

2. Most people have felt like an impostor at least some of the
    time—though feeling so does not make it true.

3. Most experts out there started out like you, with
    something to learn, something to develop, and something
    to contribute. Use this as inspiration to move forward
    with your chosen set of goals.

4. With hard work and time, you will also get there.

"People are just as wonderful as sunsets if you let them be. When I look at a sunset, I don't find myself saying 'Soften the oranges a bit on the right hand corner.' I don't try to control a sunset, I just watch with awe as it unfolds."

—Carl Rogers, PhD

Chapter 6

The Fear of Rejection

"True belonging is the spiritual practice of believing in and belonging to yourself so deeply that you can share your most authentic self with the world and find sacredness in both being part of something and standing alone."

—Brené Brown, PhD

Our need to belong is felt so deeply that rejection has been shown in research studies to be felt just as strongly as physical pain (Kross et al, 2011). Rejection threatens one of our most basic and primal needs, the need to belong. Belonging, from an evolutionary standpoint, has clear advantages—if we belonged to a group, we were more likely to survive by having access to food, shelter, and many other important resources. By being part of a group, we also had protection from predators and various other threats. Lastly, by being around a group of others, we increased our likelihood of procreating and having a family. For all of these reasons, when our belonging needs are threatened, we fear rejection, and we tend to recoil, avoid, or bolt in the other direction.

Rejection makes us feel vulnerable to a degree that few other situations can make us feel. Rejection triggers our fears of being less than, not good enough and it makes us question our own worthiness. No wonder we take such great measures to avoid feeling and experiencing it. It is brutal—it hurts us to our very core, both physically and emotionally.

Oftentimes, when we are afraid of rejection we are afraid of not fitting in. Brené Brown differentiates fitting in and belonging in the following way:

"**Fitting in** is about assessing a situation and becoming who you need to be to be accepted. **Belonging**, on the other hand, doesn't require us to change who we are; it requires us to be who we are."

Fitting in is at the shallow end of the pool of belonging; it is belonging as someone else, casting off parts or aspects of ourselves depending on the situation or social group. It is acting like a chameleon, always changing and never really showing up as our true selves. It is a way of temporarily escaping the fear of rejection, a coping strategy that comes at a high price. Because, if we never truly reveal ourselves, we can never truly be accepted and belong to anyone or anything. If we hide who we are, we are escaping, but we are not safe from fear because while we hide our true selves, we are still afraid. We are terrified that we will not be accepted. We fear that we do not belong and would not belong if we really revealed ourselves. We wonder: what if we are not well-spoken enough, attractive enough, smart enough, educated enough, good enough, or if we are fundamentally different in some blemished way? And so, we change, ever so slightly, what we believe, what we share, and what we say—and it changes us. It changes us by trapping us in a state of fear and disconnection. We become more judgmental. By being so focused on fitting in, we lose track of who we are and what we believe. And we begin to feel increasingly lonely, even when we are with people. After all—how can we feel a real sense of connection if we do not connect from a real place?

This cycle creates even more fear, more anxiety, and more perfectionism. And worst of all, it creates a wanton hollowness within us and among us. Nowhere can this be observed more readily than in the world of social media. When worth is measured in "likes" and "followers," true belonging remains hidden and fears of rejection abound. When we strive to be just like the latest celebrity, guru, or superstar athlete, we lose something important and we gain it in spades in terms of fear and anxiety about measuring up.

Am I enough? That is the fundamental question we try to answer when we compare ourselves to others. Do I really measure up? But what question are we really trying to answer here—

what are we after? In my view, those questions get us stuck in a vortex of feeling just shy of okay. These questions leave us wanting for more.

And, these lesser questions leave the more consequential questions unanswered. What do I stand for? What do I believe in? What kind of life would I like to live? With whom do I feel absolutely free to be my whole self? Who are the people who genuinely love, care, and accept me? What mark would I like to leave on this world and what gifts do I have that I can use to contribute to it? When do I hear my true voice and speak the truth even when it is uncomfortable, as it often is? These questions are often best asked and reflected upon in solitude and away from any perceived judgment that we may encounter. These are the questions that will reveal our true cores to ourselves. And, only by answering them can we really show up fully to others.

Fear-Wise Exercise: Take a few minutes and write down the answers to the questions above. Write freely as though no one else will ever read what you wrote. Write thoughtfully. If you start feeling vulnerable when you write this out—you are doing it right.

This fear of rejection, being rejected for our half-hearted beliefs, hurts. Being rejected for our true beliefs makes us emotionally vulnerable in a different way. It also provides clarity about where we do and do not belong. That clarity is important because I am certain that we all belong somewhere. That job you did not get? Perhaps it pointed you in another direction or another career path altogether. That partner it did not work out with? Maybe they led you to seek out a different kind of relationship. That social group you did not gel with? Perhaps that led you closer to finding your true tribe.

Rejection is woven into the fiber of most of our important experiences: academics, career, friendship, and romance all entail opportunities for rejection. We can opt out, aim low, and pretend to be okay just to avoid rejection, but that rarely offers us the opportunities we seek. Instead, I propose we build our rejection tolerance by accepting it as a necessary step on our journey. Rejection can be a teacher just as much about what does not work as it can about what does work. In its lessons, we can find a clearer marked path toward the goals we most value. Rather than shying away from it, I encourage us to welcome it as a beacon on the pathway to true acceptance and belonging.

Rejection is a rite of passage on your way to both getting to know yourself and to living life fully. Part of getting to know yourself is looking at those past rejections and reconsidering any negative beliefs that you have adopted. Here are some examples of what you may be looking for:

- **Unhelpful Belief:** "I am boring and people do not like to talk to me at social gatherings."

- **Helpful Belief:** "When I truly reveal myself, I have interesting things to say."

- **Unhelpful Belief:** "I am not very attractive, so I should set my sights lower when it comes to selecting a partner."

- **Helpful Belief:** "I am attractive and I should not sell myself short. I will engage with potential partners who I find attractive."

- **Unhelpful Belief:** "I am not a good speaker, so it is best to let others deliver the information instead of me."

- **Helpful Belief:** "I have things to contribute and I will let my voice be heard."

- **Unhelpful Belief:** "I am not as educated as most of my friends, so it is better that I keep my opinions to myself or I may sound stupid and make a fool of myself."

- **Helpful Belief:** "Even though I am not as educated, I try to keep informed on important subjects and I have opinions I would like to share."

- **Unhelpful Belief:** "I am not as accomplished as I would like to be, so it works better to have the conversation focus on the other person."

- **Helpful Belief:** "People would like to get to know other people, not just their accomplishments, and there are plenty of other topics to talk about."

- **Unhelpful Belief:** "I do not have a good sense of humor, so I am better off holding back when I have something to say that I think is funny so I do not embarrass myself."

- **Helpful Belief:** "Everyone can use a little humor; if I think of something funny to say, I will share it."

- **Unhelpful Belief:** "I do not know if I am a good host/hostess, so why bother having an event that I am in charge of? It will only show off my flaws."

- **Helpful Belief:** "People appreciate the challenge of hosting, and no one expects perfection—I will simply do my best."

The above set of unhelpful beliefs are grounded in the fear of rejection. They are all limiting, and they are fundamentally exhausting to carry around with you. Although they may have served you at some point in life to shield you from further rejection, they have outlived their usefulness. I encourage you to start letting go of the unhelpful beliefs that no longer serve you.

When dealing with fear of rejection, here are some FEAR-WISE truths:

1. Rejection is not a personal measure of your self-worth.

2. Rejection often has a lesson to teach us—look for it and let go of the rest.

3. Some rejection is healthy for us—it builds rejection tolerance.

4. If you are taking healthy risks and living a full life, you need to expect some rejection.

5. It is better to be rejected for your real self than to be accepted by pretending to be someone you are not.

"The most courageous act is still to think for yourself aloud."

—Coco Chanel

Chapter 7

The Fear of Our Own Voice and the Fear of Public Speaking

"How wonderful is the human voice! It is indeed the organ of the soul. The intellect of man is enthroned visibly on his forehead and in his eye, and the heart of man is written on his countenance, but the soul, the soul reveals itself in the voice only."

—Henry Wadsworth Longfellow

In the famous children's story by Hans Christian Andersen, "The Emperor's New Clothes," the king is duped into believing that he is wearing special clothes that are invisible to those who are simple-minded or stupid. While no one can actually see the clothes, his servants and advisors say nothing for fear of being

"Courage is one of my key values, and for me to feel physically, emotionally, and spiritually okay, courage *insists* that I honor it by choosing my voice over comfort."

—Brené Brown, PhD

labeled as such. When the king parades through the town in his new "clothes," only a single brave child speaks the truth, "The emperor has no clothes!"

How many times have we found ourselves in a similar situation, observing something in plain sight, but are afraid to speak the truth, whether it was to avoid being labeled incompetent or because we were afraid of becoming the subjects of ridicule or retaliation?

Our voices, they matter. They matters more than we care to admit, and we silence them far too often. Nelson Mandela famously wrote, "Fools multiply when wise men are silent." In our relationships, at school, and at work, we are expected to use our voices. In fact, in workplaces that encourage silence, both employee accident rates and error rates increase (Kim et al, 2016). And yet, we stifle our voices.

Time and again, we stop short of saying what needs to be said. We do this to avoid rejection and to "fit in" with a group, academic, or work culture. When we silence ourselves, it is at a great cost to ourselves, our relationships, and the networks we are part of.

When we silence our voices in our relationships, we deprive ourselves of having the kind of honest communication that builds the foundation for true intimacy. When we convey partial truths, we lose out on the opportunity to be fully known and understood by the people closest to us. We also create a climate of distance and unclear communication. This can lead to building unspoken resentments, unbeknownst to our intimate partners, and creating growing divides in our most intimate relationships.

When we silence our voices in the workplace, we deprive our employer of the growth our professional contributions would have had. We also deprive ourselves of building the kind of relationships with colleagues and mentors that we need to have a fulfilling work life. Finally, we create and contribute to a culture of fear and mistrust.

When we silence our voices and don't speak out on social issues, we tend to perpetuate ongoing cycles of violence or oppression. When we stay silent in the face of injustice, we tacitly give our permission with our silence. This does not mean that all of us have to lead social justice movements, just that we all participate on a personal level in some way and that our silence in these interpersonal situations speaks for itself.

I particularly love Dr. Brené Brown's reference of choosing your own voice over comfort. Choosing our own voices can be a private or public phenomenon; to me, it means trusting our inner knowledge and the inner voices that guide us in certain directions. Sometimes, trusting your voice means speaking up for what you believe and know to be true. At other times, it means quietly following your gut—either way, it implies action and often takes courage.

Fear-Wise Exercise

Write down a situation where you've withheld speaking up in your authentic voice even though it would have clear benefits. Picture the setting, down to the smallest details, including the environment, activity, and what people are wearing: write down where you are and who are with. Think about what you would like to say and write those words down. Picture a bottle of water standing on a table next to you. As you pick up that bottle and take a few sips, you start to feel a relaxing sensation in your throat—you feel that your words are becoming easier to speak. Focus on your posture and notice that your shoulders are relaxed and that you are standing up tall and straight. You speak openly and with conviction. Notice the thoughtful responses and questions that you are getting from the person or people you are speaking to. Think about their questions and answer them as easily as you just spoke. Pause here and observe the impact this exercise had on you. How do you feel? Is there a lightness anywhere in your body, do you feel a sense of being unburdened? Is this a conversation you actually would like to have? Write down any thoughts you have as a result of this exercise.

_____

_____

_____

_____

_____

_____

_____

_____

_____

_____

_____

_____

_____

_____

_____

_____

_____

_____

_____

_____

_____

_____

THE FEAR OF PUBLIC SPEAKING

"Forget conventionalisms; forget what the world thinks of you stepping out of your place; think your best thoughts, speak your best words, work your best works, looking to your own conscience for approval."

—Susan B. Anthony

One of the ways the fear of our own voice manifests is through the fear of public speaking. Repeated studies across the United States have shown this to be the number one fear people report year after year; it is surprisingly rated even higher than the fear of death. Public speaking encompasses several fears: the fear of being judged, the fear of being embarrassed or humiliated, and the fear of being rejected. To make matters even more complicated, many of us have our first encounter with public speaking in adolescence, when fears of judgment, embarrassment, and rejection are at their peak. Sometimes, this leads us to develop unhelpful beliefs about how threatening public speaking is and how good we are at doing it.

Below is a list of what some of these beliefs may sound like:

- I am just not very good at public speaking.

- I am simply too boring to be any good at this!

"There are only two types of speakers in the world. The nervous and the liars."

—Mark Twain

- I get really flustered and blush, stammer, or sweat a lot, and I get embarrassed that everyone will notice I am nervous.

- Public speakers have to be able to joke, and I do not think I am all that funny.

- The minute I start speaking, I get panicky and cannot focus on what I am saying.

- I do not like the way my voice sounds when I hear myself speak.

- Everyone will judge me and think that I am stupid.

- I will feel so embarrassed, I will never be able to live this down.

- I do not think that I am articulate enough to be any good at this.

- No one will want to be around me once they realize I do not know what I am doing.

- Every time I start speaking, I feel a lump in my throat and cannot get the words out.

- Speaking publicly will reveal that I have been putting on a show, but I really do not know what I am talking about.

In order to overcome your fear of public speaking, you will need to practice two principles: (1) change your unhelpful beliefs about your speaking abilities and feared consequences, and (2) get practice speaking.

"Years of actually getting up in front of audiences havetaught me only three lessons. One:you don't die. Two:there's no right wayto speak—only yourway. Three: it'sworth it."

—Gloria Steinem

First, write out any negative impressions you have about yourself as a speaker. Next, challenge each unhelpful belief with a new helpful belief and write out supporting details. For example, if you are telling yourself, "I am a boring speaker," write down the challenge, "I am an engaging speaker" and your supporting evidence, "My friends often laugh at my jokes."

Next, practice the new belief daily. Lastly, begin speaking in front of people as soon as you can. You are going to feel a pull to avoid this which is to be expected. Anything uncomfortable tends to bring up feelings of avoidance—it is human nature.

Begin with as small of an audience as you are comfortable with. For instance, you may want to practice in front of one close friend or

family member to start off. Ask them for honest feedback and utilize it. Begin speaking in front of larger groups as soon as you start feeling a little more confident. Please remember, true confidence will be attained only with repeated practice. Therefore, you need to make sure to gain as much experience as possible, which includes seeking out as many speaking opportunities as you can. As Hillary Clinton famously remarked: "If you are not comfortable with public speaking—and nobody starts out comfortable—you have to learn how to be comfortable. Practice. I cannot overstate the importance of practicing. Get some close family members to help evaluate you, or somebody at work that you trust."

Personally, I can really get in my head and start to overthink things when I am planning to speak in public. One of the things that had really helped me overcome this was taking improvisational comedy classes and performing in front of a live audience. One of the tenets of improvisational comedy is that mistakes do not exist—they are all fortunate accidents. This has really helped me roll with any perceived or real mistakes that often happen when speaking in front of a live audience.

If public speaking is difficult for you, check out an improvisational comedy class in your area. If none are available, classes are sometimes also offered virtually via video conferencing. It can really be a game changer when it comes to off the cuff speaking, which in my experience is all public speaking. If you think you can script everything, I encourage you to build in room for spontaneity and error—it is truly liberating to accept it.

Fear-Wise Truths

- Mistakes are part of public speaking—accepting this makes things a whole lot easier.

- Practice is truly the way to get more comfortable and to build your confidence with public speaking.

- Public speaking is a learned skill—get practice in front of people you are comfortable with first and expand your audience from there. Take as many opportunities to speak as you can.

- If you can take an improvisational comedy class—do it! This will help you build your mistake tolerance muscle.

- Your audience wants you to succeed—they are rooting for you, please join them by rooting for yourself!

Chapter 8

The Fear of Loss of Meaning

"The most terrifying fact about the universe is not that it is hostile but that it is indifferent; but if we can come to terms with this indifference and accept the challenges of life within the boundaries of death— however mutable man may be able to make them—our existence as a species can have genuine meaning and fulfillment."

—Stanley Kubrick

Whether we do so intentionally or not, we all strive to create a life filled with meaning for ourselves. That is what keeps us going during the most difficult of moments, what helps us feel energized and alive and what keeps us engaged. Conversely, we are all afraid of meaninglessness. In fact, we are truly terrified of it. To lose your sense of meaning and purpose is what many describe when they experience a severe bout of depression.

This loss of meaning is also closely tied with various addictive behaviors: alcohol and drug abuse, gambling, compulsive video game playing, shopping, internet, food, and other addictions. It feels foggy, gray, dark, and dreary—and we long for it to resolve.

We want to feel that our life stands for something, that we matter, and we fear irrelevance. It is not whether we create meaning that is the ultimate question, but how we do it. How we create meaning is uniquely personal, although I will talk about several areas that may help point us to avenues where we are likely to experience and derive meaning in our lives. First, many of us derive a sense of meaning from our family life. Our familial ties and the experiences we have in those roles, particularly the meaning associated with parenting and grandparenting roles are sources of both meaning and satisfaction. Similarly, caregiving roles for an elderly or impaired family member can also offer us a meaningful experience.

Second, our jobs can provide an abundant sense of meaning for us. Work, whether paid or volunteer, can provide a source of meaning through a sense of intellectual challenge and skill attainment. We can grow a great deal while we are mastering a career or a trade. It can also help us build a foundation of a rewarding social network that buffers stress and offers us a sense of identity and community. And, if your work relates closely with a value or values you hold, for example helping others—it also contributes to a sense of meaning in a very powerful way. Lastly, no matter how small a role you play at

"Once an individual's search for meaning is successful, it not only renders him happy but also gives him the capability to cope with suffering."

—Viktor Frankl, MD

your place of employment, the feeling of making a contribution to society can serve as an important source of meaning in and of itself.

Finally, our contributions to religious or social causes, no matter if they are paid or performed on a volunteer basis, can provide us with a great source of meaning. Whether we are passionate about saving endangered wildlife or promoting health awareness about a specific cause, these experiences are rife with meaning. I believe we all strive to connect and to be part of something and to create and contribute to a cause greater than oneself is the ultimate way to express that. Such work is rich in meaning and provides a sense of purpose.

As we create our meaning systems, it is important to note that while in general the above areas provide a source of meaning for people, your personal journey is yours alone. What you find meaningful will ultimately be unique to you. A good starting off point is to look at how you spend your time and to notice which activities or endeavors make you feel the most engaged and alive. Starting there, we can make an educated guess as to what drives those activities. For example, if you enjoy reading, it is likely that education and intellectual stimulation are values that you hold near and dear to your heart. If you practice the violin daily, then we can guess that music, its enjoyment and experience, are important to you. Take a look at the exercise on the following page to help clarify activities you enjoy.

Fear-Wise Exercise

Write down a list of five to seven activities you enjoy most.
Here are some examples. Feel free to select from the list and
add your own:

Taking walks	Drawing	Horseback riding
Pottery	Watching movies	taking care of pets
Theater	Gardening	Coding
Jogging	Puzzling	Other activities:
cooking	Doing crosswords	_____
playing music	Playing tennis	
Biking	Painting	_____
Baking	Political events	
Concerts	Soccer	_____
Yoga	Knitting	
Reading	Educational events	_____
Opera	Basketball	
Dancing	Interior design	_____
Creative writing	Religious services	
Performing comedy	Martial arts	_____
Sailing	Sewing	
Woodworking	Learning a language	_____
Attending a book club	Time with family	_____
Bowling	Volunteer work	
	Tutoring	_____

Next, write down what you enjoy about the activities. Write about what you like and how it feels to do the activity. Finally, consider whether you make enough space in your schedule to include these activities and, if not, which you would like to prioritize for inclusion first. Next, take a look of values on the next page and identify five to seven that are important to you. Try to find activities that intersect with both your interests and the values you hold in high regard.

_____

_____

_____

_____

_____

_____

_____

_____

_____

_____

_____

_____

"There is not one big cosmic meaning for all; there is only the meaning we each give to our life, an individual meaning, an individual plot, like an individual novel, a book for each person."

—Anaïs Nin

List of Your Key Values

Integrity	Freedom	Innovation
Learning	Stability	Inspiration
Spiritual life	Travel	Kindness
Adventure	Acceptance	Organization
Playfulness	Loyalty	Passion
Accomplishment	Openness	Persistence
Service	Security	Responsibility
Achievement	Humor	Sensitivity
Sincerity	Religion	Grace
Creativity	Curiosity	Success
Productivity	Reciprocity	Leadership
Friendships	Fun	Hard work
Family	Love	Individuality
Community	Generosity	Logic
Communication	Charity	Fidelity
Happiness	Commitment	Simplicity
Contribution	Compassion	Focus
Optimism	Gratitude	Enthusiasm
Harmony	Growth	Patience
Balance	Humility	Teamwork
Collaboration	Imagination	Uniqueness
Stability	Justice	Strength
Wisdom	Healing	Support
Education	Hope	Solitude
Ambition	Joy	Result-focus

Fear-Wise Plan to Increase the Sense of Meaning in Your Life

1. Acknowledge that only you can create your own path to meaning. Give up your excuses and let go of the past.

2. Creating meaning is as much about being connected to others as it is about being connected to your own sense of self. Start learning about what is important and of value to you.

3. You need to be selective about what you will include in your life—no one can do everything!

4. Areas of life where your interests intersect with your values create meaning.

5. Taking action creates meaningful paths.

Chapter 9

Our Fears at Play in Relationships

"Healthy people understand that others have the capacity to choose to end relationships and it serves as motivation for them to learn to relate in healthy and loving ways. However, when we are driven by shame, we don't just fear losing a relationship, but we live in terror that if we let anyone really get to know us, we would never be desired, pursued, or loved."

—Wendy Mahill, Growing a Passionate Heart

Relationships can stir up some of our most deeply rooted and hidden fears. We may be afraid that we will end up alone and that we are not meant to find a satisfying relationship. We may feel unlikeable, defective, unworthy, or downright unlovable. We may carry fears from our prior unsuccessful or damaging relationships with us, preventing us from entering into and developing a mutually rewarding relationship. We may be afraid to trust or to be fully open with our partner. We may hide important aspects of ourselves or our lives, afraid that we would be shunned, discarded. or labeled as defective.

We may worry about the trustworthiness of partners if we come from a background filled with secrets or betrayals. When that is the case, we may act out with excessive jealousy and become accusatory of our partners because we are afraid of them abandoning the relationship or hurting us in some other way. Alternatively, as a preemptive strike, we may leave our relationships too early in an effort to avoid becoming too attached, thereby protecting ourselves from future emotional pain that we are certain will befall us.

If we are unsure of our own self-worth, we may worry about harsh judgments, particularly if we are harshly judgmental toward our own selves. If we are not sure about our own worthiness, we may pick partners who confirm our worst fears and/or unwittingly sabotage relationships that do not align with those fears. Alternatively, we may find partners who are available and stable to be unattractive, uninteresting, or boring. We may also be hesitant to make reasonable requests and set healthy boundaries in our relationships with our time, the behaviors we accept, and how we are treated.

If we have issues with boundaries, we may worry about being swallowed up or losing our identity when we enter into a relationship. If that is our fear, we may keep a partner at a distance by being emotionally or physically unavailable. We may reveal little of ourselves or hide behind our work and other activities. On the other hand, we may want the kind of closeness that feels smothering to others and leaves our partner too little room. We may also alternate between being withholding and overly giving of ourselves.

The above fears are often a result of our life-long experience in relationships. If we felt controlled in our early close relationships, we may fear the loss of freedom that intimacy brings. If we have been hurt or abused in the past, we may not want to be emotionally vulnerable enough to enter a new relationship fully. If we grew up believing we are unworthy or unlovable, we may not be able to envision finding acceptance in a loving intimate relationship. And, if we have been betrayed by those closest to us, we may find trusting an intimate partner to be too risky.

In order to move forward and regain our relationship footing in the face of fear, we have to confront some of the damaging and destructive beliefs that we developed and still carry around with us today. Although these beliefs may have helped to protect us from hurt in the past, they have outlived their usefulness and now serve as a barrier and keep us from having healthy relationships. In order to overcome these beliefs, we have to identify exactly what beliefs we carry around today that do not serve us. Take a look at the fear list below and see if you can identify with any of the fears listed. If your fear is different, even if the difference seems slight, write it out verbatim, exactly the way it sounds when you think about it.

Below are some examples of relationship fears:

- I will feel rejected if I truly reveal myself in a relationship.

- My partner will be harsh, critical, and judgmental of my flaws.

- I am too difficult to be around or unlovable.

- I will not find the type of love I want and need.

- I am destined to be alone; I may never find a relationship.

- Once my partner gets to know me fully, they will abandon me just like many others have.

- I will feel trapped or smothered in a relationship and will no longer be able to get my own needs met.

- When I am in a relationship, I will lose sense of who I am and what I truly want and need.

- If I trust someone fully, I will be vulnerable to betrayal and getting my heart broken, and I am afraid I will not be able to recover if that happens.

- I have been hurt a lot in the past and I am afraid that I may have developed such a hard shell that I will not be able to let my guard down or get emotionally close to anyone.

- I am afraid that I will not be able to select the right partner for myself and may end up in a relationship I regret.

- I am afraid of losing my freedom and independence.

- I have too much "baggage" and I do not think a partner can handle it all.

- I have too many flaws, and I cannot imagine anyone being willing to accept them.

Once you have your fear list, I encourage you to find evidence that the fear is not true. In order to do this, find some quiet space and close your eyes and imagine a quiet, safe spot where you feel completely comfortable and have privacy. Next, imagine that you are talking with a close friend who is struggling with the same issues as you. Then, think of what you would say to them in response to the same thought. Write down the response countering your belief next to each thought you identified previously.

Below is a chart to help you keep track of the fearful beliefs and their fear-wise counterparts. Sometimes, this exercise can make us feel very emotionally tender or vulnerable. If you feel emotionally overwhelmed, please know that you do not need to do this all at once, and give yourself permission to a break from it. Come back to it when you feel ready and take as many breaks as you need.

If your relationship patterns are long-standing and if doing work on your own has brought you little or limited relief, you may want to seek out the help of a qualified mental health professional. You can ask for referrals from your physician or close friends and family members. It is important to find someone with whom you feel you can communicate openly and fully and feel that you are not being judged. For many people, this can be the first experience of having a trusting relationship that can serve as a model for building future healthy relationships.

RELATIONSHIPS

Fearful Beliefs and their Fear-Wise Counterparts

Fearful Belief	Fear-Wise Belief
I must always do everything for myself and not rely on other people—to do otherwise means I lack independence.	We are all interdependent. Even independent people need to lean on others to get things done from time to time.

If I lean on others, they will come to resent me and consider me to be a burden.	I can be aware of potential resentments and address any tension or issues as they arise. I will check in to see if my requests may be an imposition and by clarifying with the other person that they are able to meet my request.
If I ask for feedback, I will get torn to shreds and be criticized harshly, embarrassed, or humiliated.	I can use the opportunity to sharpen my ability to handle critical feedback and strengthen that feedback muscle. I also have the ability to consider only the feedback that comes from relevant and trustworthy sources.
If I ask for feedback, people will think that I am very weak or simply unsure of myself.	I have no control of what others think. I can ask for feedback in a calm and concise manner and stand to benefit from it through people who are sincere and respectful.

If I am too open with others, they will unequivocally reject or abandon me.	I can be open with others and do so gradually with those who have an accepting and non-judgmental stance.
If I commit to a relationship, my partner will certainly betray my trust just like others have in the past.	I can be more selective and choose partners who are trustworthy, honest, and dependable.
If I do not control my relationship and my partner, I will lose control.	I can only control myself, how I show up in my relationship, and what I choose to say and do.

Please use the table below to create a chart of fearful beliefs that you personally hold and a list of counter FEAR-WISE beliefs for yourself.

My Fear-Wise Beliefs

Fearful Belief	Fear-Wise Belief

"The best thing you can do is the right thing; the next best thing you can do is the wrong thing; the worst thing you can do is nothing."

—Theodore Roosevelt

Chapter 10

The Fear of Change

"When times get tough and fear sets in, think of those people who paved the way for you and those who are counting on you to pave the way for them. Never let setbacks or fear dictate the course of your life. Hold onto the possibility and push beyond the fear."

—Michelle Obama, University of California Merced Commencement Address, 2009

Change. We all yearn for it and fear it at the same time. We know the familiar can offer us a sense of comfort. Change, on the other hand, however needed and wanted, is potentially risky—it creates discomfort by its very nature. And yet, the world and our lives are forever filled with change. From the small changes we experience when we leave our houses every day to massive worldwide events and movements that take place with regularity—change is everywhere. Change is a constant, something we can count on whether we like it or not, and it is here to stay.

Our brains sometimes trick us into thinking that change will not happen. We may even use outright denial to push it away. We also tend to tell ourselves that we will have control over the change if we just negotiate with it—bargaining to keep it at bay. At times, we get mad and decide that change is something we need to protest and use our anger to fight. Lastly, we mourn the good old days and give way to sadness or depression. While this cycle can parallel any major loss and grief journey with denial, bargaining, sadness, and anger, our ultimate goal is always acceptance. Only by accepting change can we truly find a way to adjust to it and to move forward in our life.

TYPES OF CHANGE

Sudden, Unanticipated Change

Many times, change is thrust upon us suddenly, without notice. In March of 2020, we all felt the impact of the COVID-19 pandemic as we were forced to change our lives suddenly and drastically due to the mandated worldwide quarantines aimed to mitigate the public health risk. Suddenly, many of us found ourselves unable to work or working remotely by telecommuting. We also had to limit our travel and social interactions by staying home as much as possible—something that many of us thought would be unbearable prior to the pandemic. And yet, life went on—we adjusted and we learned to thrive in spite of it.

Many of us picked up new skills, found a goldmine of time we could spend with our children or families, and learned to be creative with our extra time. We also found innovative and fun ways to connect with our loved ones using various technology tools. The lesson was that we are all capable of change and many of us begin to thrive once we adjust.

In science, chaos theory states that the universe is always leaning toward disorder. This means that the world as we know it is constantly changing and presenting new challenges. If we accept this process as the natural order of the universe we do not have to be afraid of it. It is a law of nature and is a constant. As much as we may prefer for things to be orderly, tidy, and predictable, the universe is built otherwise. And so, we must develop tools to manage and thrive in the face of evolving circumstances.

As a psychologist, I am heartened and amazed by this ability we all possess—the psychological term for this is posttraumatic growth, or growth we experience as a result of going through psychologically challenging adversity. Posttraumatic growth theory was developed by psychologists Tedeschi and Calhoun, and it posits that following a psychologically difficult adjustment, growth is possible in the following five areas:

- Appreciation of life.

- Relationships with others.

- New possibilities in life.

- Personal strength.

- Spiritual change.

Posttraumatic growth is not the same as resilience, but it may actually create more resilience in someone who can re-evaluate their belief system. I think this speaks to our innate capacity to draw on our internal resources in the face of challenges and setbacks.

Planned Change

Sometimes, planned change is warranted and required. We would like to change our careers, go back to work, begin new hobbies, go back to school, or leave relationships. This type of change often shows up along with fear of decision-making. We tend to know what we want to do, but we stall and procrastinate with regards to committing to this choice. Planned change is often easier if we think of it as a series of steps. For example, going back to school might involve the following series of steps:

- Researching universities that offer a degree in your area of study.

- Planning for how you will pay for the cost of your education (self-funding or applying for scholarships, grants, or loans).

- Selecting several schools or universities to apply to.

- Filling out and submitting the necessary applications for admission.

- Studying for and completing any necessary pre-admission testing and/or coursework.

- Selecting one of the schools or universities from those you were admitted to.

- Finalizing your acceptance paperwork and plans.

When you break a goal into its components, the bigger change often seems less overwhelming.

Behavioral Habit Change

Another type of change happens when you are trying to build a new habit. It can seem overwhelming if you are trying to break a longstanding pattern. Let's use deciding to eat less sugary sweets as an example.

Up until now, you may be used to having a slice of cake with dinner. Now, you decide that for the benefit of your health, you will have fruit instead. In order to be successful, you will need to commit to making this choice on a daily basis. To set yourself up for success, you decide not to purchase cake or similar pastries so that you are not tempted to have them when you are home. You also decide to prepare by purchasing fruit and slicing it up as part of your weekly food preparation. Additionally, you allow yourself to miss the feeling of eating cake and acknowledge that enjoying fruit as your dessert will take getting used to.

After a few days, you notice that your cravings subside, and you enjoy having fruit for dessert. What you have done is gradually substituted a healthier habit in place of a less desirable one—this is how habits really change.

Emotional Response Change

Changing your emotional responses is often the toughest type of change. We may realize that we need to approach situations with more equanimity and a less emotional stance, but when push comes to shove, we find ourselves losing our cool and reverting back to the old patterns.

Behaviors are driven by beliefs and so are our emotional responses. When we are trying to change the expression of our emotional response, we are really trying to change a behavior that is driven by a belief. Often, we respond more intensely when we are taking the situation personally, are driven by the desire to win the argument or to be right, or we are making faulty assumptions about the intention of another person's behavior toward us. At times, these factors are also compounded by a belief that we have to address the situation immediately, express ourselves fully, and/or punish the perceived wrong-doer for their transgression. Unfortunately, this usually results in escalating the situation rather than creating the resolution that we seek.

When trying to create emotional change, it is important to go slowly. Start with observing your body. When you feel yourself getting emotionally flooded, take a break—get some water or create another opportunity to walk away from the situation and to physically recalibrate. Once you feel calmer, decide not to take the situation personally and stick to the facts. What behavior upset you and what would improve the situation? Next, decide if what you are after is realistic. For example, if you are looking for an apology from the chief executive of a major corporation regarding an issue you have with working overtime all week—your request is likely unrealistic. On the other hand, letting your immediate supervisor know that you have to leave the office by six p.m. every Monday and Wednesday due to commitments you have is probably realistic.

When you are creating emotional change, deciding how you would like to communicate is key. Typically, the calmer your demeanor is, the louder your message. Additionally, you can try to explain the situation in as few words as possible. Have a clear request of the other person: "I would like to get assistance with graphic design projects because my workload has doubled in the last six months. I have some ideas and would like to run them by you. When do you have time to meet to meet this week?" This request is clear because it asks for a meeting and explains the reason for it as well as setting up a time frame. The clearer and more specific you are, the more likely the other person will be open and receptive to your request.

Fear-Wise Truths

- The fear-wise accept that change is a constant.

- The fear-wise focus on things that you do control when facing change. For example: You may not have control over the company downsizing and eliminating your job, but you do have control over looking for another job, networking, calling recruiters, and updating your resume.

- The fear-wise create anchors in an ever-changing world. Embracing change means balancing it with things that keep you feeling steady and balanced. This means creating routines that work for you at work and in your personal life.

- The fear-wise know when to seek support, such as when they are feeling stressed or overwhelmed.

- The fear-wise know when to set appropriate boundaries, decide not to over-commit, and take breaks.

Chapter 11

Fear and Danger

Fear. It can be a gut-wrenching, chest-gripping false alarm, or it can be a blaring danger signal that can save your life. I did not have time to think through every possibility that day. I just knew I had to act.

One spring day a few years ago, I was involved in a minor fender bender on a major expressway. My vehicle was the last car in a three-car collision. I looked in the rearview mirror at my daughter's face in the back seat and I knew that I had to get her out of that car as fast as possible. We quickly made our way to get into the car of the person in front of ours, and just moments later, our empty car was demolished by an eighteen-wheeler barreling down the highway.

It was fear that gave me the courage to ask another driver for assistance and what kept myself, and my daughter out of harm's way that day. Having never been in that situation before, it was

not life experience that helped save my life that day, it was the
call of fear. These moments are split-second decision moments.
They are the listen-to-your-gut moments, and they warn us of
impending danger that can save our lives if we heed their call.

In his comprehensive book, *The Gift of Fear: And Other Survival
Signals That Protect Us from Violence*, Gavin de Becker, a security
specialist for major corporations and public figures, outlines
how our fear signals can protect us from violence. Unlike worry
and anxiety which keep us guessing in hypothetical scenarios,
fear provides clear guidance when it comes to preserving
our safety. Trusting that intuitive voice can often mean the
difference between life and death.

Our intuition has been finely tuned through our life experience
and refined moment-to-moment to protect us from danger and
it does not lead us astray. According to de Becker, "The intuitive
signal of the highest order, the one with the greatest urgency,
is fear; accordingly, it should always be listened to." Other
messengers of intuition that can protect us from danger in
order of urgency are "apprehension, suspicion, then hesitation,
doubt, gut feelings, hunches, curiosity, anxiety, wonder, humor,
nagging feelings, persistent thoughts, and physical sensations."
These are important signals we need to heed in order to keep
ourselves safe from dangerous situations and/or violence.

The Fear-Wise Truths

- Trust your sense of fear—it can be life preserving. You do not need to know why you are walking away. You will often be able to figure it out after the fact.

- Life preserving fear is not about what other people think or your reputation.

- Fear that is life preserving happens in the moment. Learn to differentiate it from anxiety or worry about what will happen in the future.

Chapter 12

Everyone Is Afraid and Everyone Has Courage

"Courage is about learning how to function despite the fear, to put aside your instincts to run or give in completely to the anger born from fear. Courage is about using your brain and your heart when every cell of your body is screaming at your to fight or flee—and then following through on what you believe is the right thing to do."

—Jim Butcher

Being courageous does not mean being without fear, it means moving forward while being afraid. Often, it feels like you are flying without a net and it always means feeling more energized and enlivened in the process. Why would we choose to do this when we can cuddle up in the nook of safety? Because not to do so would leave us with lives that feels lackluster, that feel wanting, and that lead to regrets for the roads we have not pursued, the challenges we did not take on, and the risks we did not face.

In order to be courageous, there are five steps we must take:

1. We have to be willing to give up the façade of safety—and it is a façade because in not taking the necessary risk, we risk something else altogether. We risk giving up on an important value, a key mission, or a great adventure. The only way forward is through action.

2. We need to tap into our own truth and our authentic values. In order to do this, we need to be willing to be honest with ourselves about what really matters to us. We have to create the personal space to discover this among the many competing "shoulds" we may feel we are bound to—they are just noise keeping us from finding our singing voice.

3. We have to create meaning. When we pursue life in accordance to our values, moving forward becomes more fluid. When you know that painting is what makes your heart sing, picking up that paintbrush day after day becomes seamless. Find what makes your heart sing—and do it!

4. Take a leap. Action is what defines courage. You can wait around for the fear to pass, for some sense of safety to suddenly descend, or you can take action now, because

otherwise you may be waiting forever. Most of the time, we have to take steps while being afraid, sometimes when we are outright terrified.

5. Have faith. We have to have faith to keep going and to have courage when it starts waning and we will need to take another leap. Having courage is not a straightforward path; it is picking up again and again in the face of fear and obstacles. Trust yourself and trust your internal resources to get you through. Most importantly, please remember that even when it feels like it, you are not doing this alone. Everywhere in the world, in your city and your neighborhood, maybe somewhere just a few feet away, there is someone else fighting that same battle. And, although you may not know who they are or the details of their particular fight, you can be united in the knowledge that you are in this together.

Acknowledgements

In writing this book, there are many people who deserve my sincerest thank you. Writing, although a solitary pursuit, requires the input, support, and collaboration of so many others. Although I cannot thank everyone by name here, please know that I appreciate your support nevertheless.

First and foremost, I would like to thank my editor Brenda Knight for her tireless oversight of this project. I would also like to thank the entire team at Mango Publishing for helping my manuscript evolve and materialize into a published book. I truly appreciate the backing of your fantastic team to help publish and promote it.

To Dr. John Duffy, thank you for being such a great sounding board for my ideas as I worked and reworked this manuscript.

I would like to thank my entire family. Thank you to my parents for your love and support. To my daughter Maya, thank you for the joy you bring and the unbridled enthusiasm you have about having a mom who is an author.

To my husband Alex, thank you for the room you create to help me take the time and energy necessary for this undertaking. Thank you for your humor and support while I work and rework my ideas and take necessary time to write out and edit them. This book would not be possible without you.

Finally, to my clients, thank you for allowing me to witness your journeys as you overcome your fears and teach me every day about what courage truly means!

References

Chapter 1

Merriam-Webster Dictionary online.

Beck, Aaron (1987). Anxiety Disorders and Phobias (p. 9).

Adolphs, Ralph (2012). Curr Biol 2013 January 21;23 R79-R93, doi 10.1016/j.cub.2012.11.055

Chapter 6

Kross, Ethan; Berman, Marc G.; Mischel, Walter; Smith, Edward E.; Wager, Tor D. "Social rejection shares somatosensory representations with physical pain." Proc Natl Acad Sci U S A. 2011 Apr 12; 108(15): 6270–6275.

Chapter 7

Kim, Yangho; Park, Jung sun; and Park, Mijin. "Creating a Culture of Prevention in Occupational Safety and Health Practice." https://www.sciencedirect.com/science/article/pii/S2093791116000093#bbib3

Chapter 10

Growth After Trauma; Why are Some People More Resilient than Others—and Can It be Taught? Lorna Collier. November 2016, Vol 47, No. 10, p. 48. https://www.apa.org/monitor/2016/11/growth-trauma

Resources

10% Happier: How I Tamed the Voice in My Head, Reduced Stress Without Losing My Edge, and Found Self-Help That Actually Works—--A True Story, Dan Harris

13 Things Mentally Strong People Don't Do:, Take Back your Power, Embrace Change, Face Your Fears, and Train Your Brain for Happiness and Success, Amy Morin, PhD

Anxiety and Worry: How to learn to overcome anxiety, fears, intrusive thoughts, worry, depression, stop overthinking, with C. B. T., meditation exercises, and positive affirmations to raise self-esteem, Kristin Winters

Anxiety Disorders and Phobias: A Cognitive Perspective, Aaron T. Beck, MD

Anxiety Free: Unravel Your Fears Before They Unravel You, Robert L. Leahy, PhD

Authentic Happiness: Using the New Positive Psychology to Realize Your Potential for Lasting Fulfillment, Martin E. P. Seligman, PhD

Badass Ways to End Anxiety & Stop Panic Attacks!: A counterintuitive approach to recover and regain control of your life, Geert Verschaeve

Boundaries for Your Soul: How to Turn Your Overwhelming Thoughts and Feelings into Your Greatest Allies, Allison Cook Ph. D. and Kimberly Miller, M. Th., LMFT

Boundaries in Dating: How Healthy Choices Grow Healthy Relationships,
Dr. Henry Cloud and Dr. John Townsend

*Boundaries in Marriage: Understanding the Choices That Make or Break
Love Relationships*, Dr. Henry Cloud and Dr. John Townsend

*Boundaries Undated and Expanded Edition: When to Say Yes, How
to Say No to Gain Control of Your Life*, Dr. Henry Cloud and Dr.
John Townsend

Boundaries with Kids: How Healthy Choices Grow Healthy Kids, Dr.
Henry Cloud and Dr. John Townsend

*Braving the Wilderness: The Quest for True Belonging and the Courage to
Stand Alone*, Brené Brown, PhD, LMSW

*Cognitive Behavioral Therapy Made Simple: 10 Strategies for Managing
Anxiety, Depression, Anger, Panic, and Worry*, Seth J. Gillihan, PhD

*Conquer Anxiety Workbook for Teens: Find Peace from Worry, Panic,
Fear, and Phobias*, Tabatha Chansard, PhD

*Crucial Confrontations: Tools for Resolving Broken Promises, Violated
Expectations, and Bad Behavior*, Kerry Patterson, Joseph Grenny,
Ron Mc Millan and Al Switzler.

Crucial Conversations: Tools for Talking When Stakes Are High, Kerry
Patterson, Joseph Grenny, Ron McMillan, and Al Switzler

Dare to Lead: Brave Work. Tough Conversations. Whole Hearts. , Brené
Brown, PhD, LMSW

Daring Greatly: How the Courage to Be Vulnerable Transforms the Way We Live, Love, Parent, and Lead, Brené Brown, PhD, LMSW PhD, LMSW

Don't Feed the Monkey Mind: How to Stop the Cycle of Anxiety, Fear, and Worry, Jennifer Shannon, LMFT

Don't Panic: Taking Control of Anxiety Attacks, Reid Wilson, PhD

Emotional Agility: Get Unstuck, Embrace Change, and Thrive in Work and In Life, Susan David, PhD

Emotional Intelligence: Why It Can Matter More Than IQ, Daniel Goleman

Fear and Other Uninvited Guests: Tackling the Anxiety, Fear, and Shame that Keep Us From Optimal Living and Loving, Harriet Lerner

Fear: Essential Wisdom for Getting Through the Storm, Thich Nhat Hanh

Feel the Fear and Do it Anyway:, Dynamic Techniques to Turn Fear, Indecision, and Anger into Action, Power, and Love, Susan Jeffers, PhD

Freedom from Obsessive Compulsive Disorder: A Personalized Recovery Program for Living with Uncertainty, Updated Edition, Jonathan Grayson, PhD

Getting Past No: Negotiating in Difficult Situations, William Ury

Getting to Yes with Yourself: How to Get What You Truly Want, William Ury

Getting to Yes: Negotiating Agreement Without Giving In, Roger Fisher, William Ury, and Bruce Patterson

Hope and Help for Your Nerves, Claire Weekes, MD

How to Be an Imperfectionist: The New Way to Self-Acceptance, Fearless Living, and Freedom From Perfectionism, Stephen Guise

How to Be Yourself: Quiet Your Inner Critic and Quiet Your Social Anxiety, Ellen Hendriksen, PhD

How to Overcome Fear of Flying: A Practical Guide to Change the Way You Think about Airplanes, Fear and Flying: Learn to Manage Takeoff, Turbulence, Flying over Water, Anxiety and Panic Attacks, Captain, Ron Nielsen

I Hear You:, The Surprisingly Simple Skill Behind Extraordinary Relationships, Michael S. Sorensen

Learned Optimism: How to Change Your Mind and Your Life, Martin E. P. Seligman, PhD

Make Your Bed: Little Things That Can Change Your Life...and Maybe the World, Admiral William H. McRaven

Man's Search for Meaning, Viktor E. Frankl, MD

Mind Over Mood, Second Edition: Change How You Feel by Changing the Way You Think, Dennis Greenberger Ph. D., Christine A. Padesky, PhD

Mindset:; The New Psychology of Success, Carol Dweck, PhD.

Negotiating for Success: Essential Strategies and Skills, George J. Seidel

Negotiating the Nonnegotiable: How to Resolve Your Most Emotionally Charged Conflicts, Daniel Shapiro

Never Good Enough: How to use Perfectionism to Your Advantage Without Letting Iit Ruin Your Life, Monica Basco, PhD

Nice Girls Don't Get the Corner Office: Unconscious Mistakes Women Make That Sabotage Their Careers (A NICE GIRLS Book), Lois P. Frankel, PhD

Nice Girls Don't Speak Up or Stand Out: How to Make Your Voice Heard, Your Point Known, and Your Presence Felt, Lois P. Frankel, PhD

Nice Girls Just Don't Get It: 99 Ways to Win the Respect You Deserve, the Success You've Earned, and the Life You Want, Lois P. Frankel, PhD

Not Nice: Stop People Pleasing, Staying Silent, & Feeling Guilty…and Start Speaking Up, Saying No, Asking Boldly, and Unapologetically Being Yourself, Dr. Aziz Gazipura

Optimal Outcomes: Free Yourself from Conflict at Work, at Home, and in Life, Jennifer Goldman-Wetzler, PhD

Overcoming Health Anxiety: Letting Go of Your Fear of Illness, Catherine Owens, PhD and Martin M. Anthony, PhD

Overcoming Unwanted Intrusive Thoughts: A C. B. T. Based Guide to Getting over Frightening, Obsessive, or Disturbing Thoughts, Sally. M. Winston, Psy. D. and Martin N. Seif, PhD

Panic Free: The 10-Day Program to End Panic, Anxiety, and Claustrophobia, Tom Bunn

Parenting the New Teen in the Age of Anxiety: A Complete Guide to Your Child's Stressed, Depressed, Expanded, Amazing Adolescence, John G. Duffy, Psy. D.

Performing Under Pressure: The Science of Doing Your Best When It Matters Most, Hendrie Weisinger and J. P. Pawliw-Fry

Practicing Mindfulness: 75 Essential Meditations to Reduce Stress, Improve Mental Health, and Find Peace in the Everyday, Matthew Sockolov

Prescriptions Without Pills: For Relief from Depression, Anger, Anxiety, and More, Susan Heitler, PhD

Presence, Bringing Your Boldest Self to Your Biggest Challenges, Amy Cuddy

Reinventing Your Life: The Breakthrough Program to End Negative Behavior and Feel Great Again, Jeffrey M. Young, PhD and Janet Klosko, PhD

Soar: The Breakthrough Treatment For Fear Of Flying, Tom Bunn

Speak With Fear:, Go From a Nervous, Nauseated Sweaty Speaker to an Excited Energized and Passionate Presenter, Mike Acker

Staring at the Sun: Overcoming the Terror of Death, Irwin D. Yalom, MD

Stop Anxiety From Stopping You, The Breakthrough Program for Overcoming Panic and Social Anxiety, Helen Odessky, Psy. D.

Stopping the Noise in Your Head : the New Way to Overcome Anxiety and Worry, Reid Wilson, PhD

The 7 Habits of Highly Effective People: Powerful Lessons in Personal Change, Stephen R. Covey

The Anxiety and Phobia Workbook, Edmund J. Bourne, PhD

The Anxiety and Phobia Workbook: The Cognitive Behavioral Solution, David A. Clark PhD and Aaron T. Beck, MD

The Anxiety Skills Workbook: Simple CBT and Mindfulness Strategies for Overcoming Anxiety, Fear, and Worry, Stephan G. Hoffman, PhD

The Anxiety Toolkit: Strategies for Fine-Tuning Your Mind and Moving Past Your Stuck Points, Allison Boyes, PhD

The Anxiety Workbook: A 7-Week Plan to Overcome Anxiety, Stop Worrying, and End Panic, Arlin Cuncic, MA

The Anxiety, Worry and & Depression Workbook: 65 Exercises to Improve Mood and Feel Better, Jennifer L. Abel, PhD

The Anxious Thoughts Workbook: Skills to Overcome the Unwanted Intrusive Thoughts That Drive Anxiety, Obsessions, and Depression, David A. Clark, PhD

The Art of Fear: Why Conquering Fear Won't Work and What to Do Instead, Kristen Ulmer

The Art Of Saying NO: How To Stand Your Ground, Reclaim Your Time And Energy, And Refuse To Be Taken For Granted (Without Feeling Guilty!), Damon Zahariades

The Artist's Way: A Spiritual Path to Higher Creativity, Julia Cameron

The Big Leap:, Conquer Your Hidden Fear and Take Life to The Next Level, Gay Henricks

The Chemistry of Calm: A Powerful, Drug-Free Plan to Quiet Your Fears and Overcome Your Anxiety, Henry Emmons, MD

The Cognitive Behavioral Therapy Workbook for Panic Attacks, Elena Welsh, PhD

The Cognitive Behavioral Workbook for Anxiety: A Step By Step Program, William J. Knauss, Ed. D. and Jon Carlson, PsyD, ABPP

The Confidence Gap: A Guide to Overcoming Fear and Self Doubt, Russ Harris

The Dialectical Behavior Therapy Skills Workbook for Anxiety: Breaking Free from Worry, Panic, PTSD, and Other Anxiety Symptoms, Alexanderdra L. Chapman, PhD, R. Psych., Kim L. Gratz PhD, and Matthew T. Tull, PhD

The Dialectical Behavior Therapy Skills Workbook: Practical DBT Exercises for Learning Mindfulness, Interpersonal Effectiveness, Emotion Regulation, and Distress Tolerance, Matthew McKay Ph. D., Jeffrey C. Wood, PsyD, and Jeffrey Brantley, MD

The Fear of Flying Workbook: Overcome Your Anticipatory Anxiety and Develop Skills For Flying with Confidence, David Carbonell, PhD

The Four Agreements: A Practical Guide to Personal Freedom (A Toltec Wisdom Book), Don Miguel Ruiz

The Generalized Anxiety Disorder Workbook: A Comprehensive CBT Guide for Coping with Uncertainty, Worry, and Fear, Melisa Robichaud, PhD and Miechel J. Douglas Dugas, PhD

The Gift of Fear: And Other, *Survival Signals That Protect Us From Violence,* Gavin De Becker

The Gifts of Imperfection: Let Go of Who You Think You're Supposed to Be and Embrace Who You Are, Brené Brown, PhD, LMSW, LMSW

The Highly Sensitive Person in Love: Understanding and Managing Relationships When the World Overwhelms You, Elaine N. Aron, PhD

The Highly Sensitive Person: How to Thrive When the World Overwhelms You, Elaine N. Aron, PhD

The Joy Of Imperfection: A Stress-Free Guide To Silencing Your Inner Critic, Conquering Perfectionism, and Becoming The Best Version Of Yourself!, Daman Zahariades

The Joy of Missing Out: Live More by Doing Less, Tonya Dalton

The Mindfulness and Acceptance Workbook for Anxiety: A Guide to Breaking Free from Anxiety, Phobias, and Worry Using Acceptance and Commitment Therapy, John P. Forsyth, Ph. D. and Georg H. Eifert, PhD

The Mindfulness and Acceptance Workbook for Social Anxiety and Shyness: Using Acceptance and Commitment Therapy to Free Yourself from Fear and Reclaim Your Life, Jan E. Fleming, MD, Nancy L. Kocovski, PhD, and Zindel V. Segal, PhD

The Mindfulness Workbook for Anxiety: The 8-Week Solution to Help You Manage Anxiety, Worry & Stress, Tanya J. Petersen, MS, NCC

The Mindfulness Workbook for OCD: A Guide to Overcoming Obsessions and Compulsions Using Mindfulness and Cognitive Behavioral Therapy, Jonathan Hershfield, MFT and Tom Corboy, MFT

The OCD Workbook: Your Guide to Breaking Free from Obsessive-Compulsive Disorder, Bruce M. Hyman, PhD, LCSW and Cherlene Pedrick, RN

The Panic Workbook for Teens: Breaking the Cycle of Fear, Worry, and Panic Attacks, Debra Kissen, PhD, Bari Goldman Cohen, PhD, and Kathi Fine Abitbol, PhD

The Perfectionism Workbook: Proven Strategies to End Procrastination, Accept Yourself, and Achieve Your Goals, Taylor Newendorp, MA, LCPC

The Power of Habit:, Why We Do What We Do in Life and In Business, Charles Duhigg

The Power of Now: A Guide to Spiritual Enlightenment, Eckhart Tolle

The Power of Two Workbook: Communication Skills for a Strong & Loving Marriage, Susan Heitler, Ph. D. and Abigail Hirsch, PhD

The Relationship Cure: A 5 Step Guide to Strengthening Your Marriage, Family, and Friendships, John M. Gottman, Ph. D. and Joan DeClaire

The Relaxation and Stress Reduction Workbook, Martha Davis Ph. D., Elizabeth Robbins Eshelman M. S. W. and Matthew McKay, PhD

The Self Care Prescription: Powerful Solutions to Manage Stress, Reduce Anxiety & Increase Wellbeing, Robyn Gobin

The Self Confidence Workbook: A Guide to Overcoming Self-Doubt and Improving Self-Esteem, Barbara Markaway, PhD and Celia Ampel

The Seven Principles for Making Marriage Work: A Practical Guide from the Country's Foremost Relationship Expert, John M. Gottman Ph. D. and Nan Silver

The Shyness & Social Anxiety Workbook: Proven Techniques for Overcoming Your Fears, Martin M. Antony Ph. D. and Richard P. Swinson MD

The Stress-Proof Brain: Master Your Emotional Response to Stress Using Mindfulness and Neuroplasticity, Melanie Greenberg, PhD

The Upside of Stress: Why Stress Is Good for You, and How to Get Good at It, Kelly McGonnigal, PhD

The War of Art, Steven Pressfield

The Worry Trick: How Your Brain Tricks You into Expecting the Worst and What You Can Do about It, David Carbonell, PhD

Victory Favors the Fearless: How to Defeat the 7 Fears That Hold You Back (Sports for the Soul), Darrin Donnelly

What Makes Love Last?: How to Build Trust and Avoid Betrayal, John M. Gottman, PhD and Nan Silver

When Panic Attacks: The New Drug-Free Anxiety Therapy That Can Change Your Life, David D. Burns, MD

When Perfect Isn't Good Enough: Strategies for Coping with Perfectionism, Martin M. Anthony, Ph. D. and Richard P. Swinson MD

Why Marriages Succeed or Fail: And How You Can Make Yours Last,
John M. Gottman, PhD and Nan Silver

About the Author

 Dr. Helen Odessky is a highly sought-after clinical psychologist, speaker, coach, and anxiety expert. She is the author of the #1 bestselling book *Stop Anxiety from Stopping You*. She has been working with individuals, teens, and couples for over fifteen years. Dr. Odessky sees clients in her anxiety-focused practice in Chicago. She is a highly sought-after public speaker and regularly speaks to corporate clients through her speaker's bureau work such as KPMG, Bank of Montreal, and Bank of America. Dr. Odessky regularly blogs on anxiety and communicates regularly to her growing base of followers on Facebook, Instagram, LinkedIn, and Twitter.

Mango Publishing, established in 2014, publishes an eclectic list of books by diverse authors—both new and established voices—on topics ranging from business, personal growth, women's empowerment, LGBTQ studies, health, and spirituality to history, popular culture, time management, decluttering, lifestyle, mental wellness, aging, and sustainable living. We were recently named 2019 and 2020's #1 fastest growing independent publisher by *Publishers Weekly.* Our success is driven by our main goal, which is to publish high quality books that will entertain readers as well as make a positive difference in their lives.

Our readers are our most important resource; we value your input, suggestions, and ideas. We'd love to hear from you—after all, we are publishing books for you!

Please stay in touch with us and follow us at:

Facebook: Mango Publishing
Twitter: @MangoPublishing
Instagram: @MangoPublishing
LinkedIn: Mango Publishing
Pinterest: Mango Publishing
Newsletter: mangopublishinggroup.com/newsletter

Join us on Mango's journey to reinvent publishing, one book at a time.